The Mediterranean Diet for Beginners

The Complete Guide - 60 Easy Slow Cooker Recipes, Diet Meal Plan and Cookbook to Lose Weight

Table of Contents

INTRODUCTION

The Mediterranean Diet plan Accomplishes a Target of Only 1200 Calories a Day:

Mediterranean Breakfast - Greek Yoghurt with Blueberries and Chopped Pistachios (449 calories)

Mediterranean Snack (152 calories)

Mediterranean Dinner (356 calories)

3 Ways to Increase Your Chance of Losing Weight on a Mediterranean Diet.

1. Eat very early in the morning

2. Serve vegetables cooked in olive oil as your main meal for the day

3. Drink lots of water, and coffee, tea, and (for adults) wine.

How the Mediterranean Diet can Assist

with Weight Reduction

Fruit salad

Sardines on Toast

Avocado Baked Eggs

Frittata

Tostadas

Traditional Moroccan Bread with Honey

Breakfast bake

Sweet potato hash with kale

Scrambled eggs with feta and spinach

Zucchini and Goat Cheese Frittata

Savory Fava Beans With Warm Pita Bread

- Tuscan Chicken Skillet
- Barley and Roasted Tomato Risotto
- Mediterranean-Style Grilled Salmon
- Polenta With Roasted Mediterranean Vegetables
- Vegetable and Garlic Calzone
- Bean Salad with Balsamic Vinaigrette
- Braised Kale With Cherry Tomatoes
- Roasted Red Pepper With Feta Salad
- Grilled Chicken + Dill Greek Yogurt Sauce
- Kale and Feta One-Pot Pasta
- Mediterranean Tacos
- Skinny Bruschetta Chicken
- Mediterranean Greek Salad
- Penne with Shrimp
- Avocado Egg Salad
- Garlic Mushroom Kebabs
- Mediterranean Salmon
- Warm Olives with Rosemary
- Mediterranean Grilled Vegetable Tagine
- Zucchini Noodles With Poached Egg Topper
- African Heritage Mango & Papaya After-Chop
- Creamy Mediterranean Paninis
- Mediterranean Skewers with Bloody Mary Vinaigrette
- Vegetable Omelet
- Lemon Scones
- Slow Cooker Mediterranean Beef Stew with Rosemary and Balsamic Vinegar
- Mediterranean Zucchini Sticks

- Grouper with tomato-olive sauce
- Mediterranean-Style Grilled Salmon
- Artichokes Alla Romana
- Beet Walnut Salad
- Fresh Tomato Crostini
- Grilled Chicken and Grape Skewers
- Kale, Cannellini and Farro Stew
- Mediterranean Chicken Pasta
- Mediterranean Tuna Salad with a Zesty Dijon Mustard Vinaigrette
- Mediterranean Breakfast Quinoa
- Easy Mediterranean Fish
- Sicilian Spaghetti
- Caprese-Style Portobellos
- Mediterranean Seafood Grill with Skordalia
- Portobello Mushrooms with Mediterranean Stuffing
- Mediterranean Breakfast Couscous
- Chicken-Garbanzo Salad
- Black-eyed Pea Fritters From West Africa
- Yucatan Bean And Pumpkin Seed Appetizer
- Mediterranean Halibut Sandwiches
- Conclusion

Thank you

INTRODUCTION

The *Mediterranean Diet* is the world's oldest diet. And not only is it ancient, it is also healthy and very effective for weight reduction.

According to the PREDIMED study (*Prevention with Mediterranean Diet*), which was a large Spanish primary prevention trial comprising 7,447 Spanish participants between the ages of 55 years and 80 years, of whom 58% women, the *Mediterranean Diet* helps people lose more weight as compared to a low-fat diet. The participants were generally healthy, but at a high risk for cardiovascular disease. These results were confirmed by another study which was published in 2008 in the *New England Journal of Medicine*.

These results suggest that at last it is time to say goodbye to boring low-fat food. You are now able to lose weight on a healthily delicious diet

The Mediterranean Diet plan Accomplishes a Target of Only 1200 Calories a Day:

Mediterranean Breakfast - Greek Yoghurt with Blueberries and Chopped Pistachios (449 calories)

Mix 1 cup each of blueberries and full cream Greek Yogurt in a breakfast bowl.

Sprinkle 2 tbsp. of chopped pistachios on top for taste.

Enjoy!

Mediterranean Lunch (255 calories)

> 4 cups of spinach;
>
> 1 tsp. olive oil;
>
> 1 chopped up tomato;
>
> ¼ cup sliced cucumber;
>
> 3 tbsp. crumble feta;
>
> 5 large roasted shrimp;
>
> 2 tbsp. balsamic vinaigrette

Toss all ingredients together in a medium sized bowl and enjoy!

Mediterranean Snack (152 calories)

¼ cup of almonds contain 152 calories. Do not take more than that, since increasing the quantity would also increase the total calorie count for the day.

Mediterranean Dinner (356 calories)

-Sauté 1 cup broccoli, using 1 tsp olive oil.

-Pair with 4 oz. white fish, cooked with oregano, and ½ cup cooked quinoa.

Enjoy!

This one-day meal plan day will provide 1212 calories. However, with the *Mediterranean Diet* you do not have to stress about calories. If you feel famished, then increase your calorie intake. Also remember that you have to add calories before each gym session

3 Ways to Increase Your Chance of Losing Weight on a Mediterranean Diet.

1. Eat very early in the morning

Traditionally, Mediterranean people eat their lunch around 1pm to 3 pm. If you have you breakfast very early in the morning, you will be able to control yourself and not over-eat later in the day. According to a Spanish research study, "individuals that eat their main meal before 3 pm are bound to lose more weight."

2. Serve vegetables cooked in olive oil as your main meal for the day

Using olive oil to cook your vegetables works magic. Not only does a vegetable meal rich in olive oil and tomatoes great satisfaction, it also includes 3-4 servings of vegetables in one meal.

Such a meal is low in carbs, and provides enough calories to sustain you all day long. Combine it with a delicious feta cheese, and you're good to go. Another benefit of eating vegetables as your maim meal for the day is keeping you alert all day, and keeping away the that is a bother with meals rich in carbohydrates.

3. Drink lots of water, and coffee, tea, and (for adults) wine.

I certain countries, such as the U.S., drinking milk during meals is a generally acceptable habit. However, it is not advisable. The vast majority of Mediterranean dairy intake is derived from yogurt and cheese. Make sure that you eat mainly calories provided by solid food and not liquids.

The same goes for juice. You don't not really need the juice. It is advisable to eat fruit rather than drink juice. Fruit contains a whole lot of nutrients and fibers.

Note: Coffee and wine are both crucial to the <u>Mediterranean Diet</u>, but never as a replacement for water.

How the Mediterranean Diet can Assist with Weight Reduction

Since the Mediterranean Diet focuses on the quality of food rather than the quality, it is important to remember that it also prohibits the intake of certain food items. This is done to ensure early and proper results.

Food items that has to be consumed while following the Mediterranean Diet

Tubers: turnips, yarns, sweet potatoes, potatoes, etc.

Vegetables: tomatoes, cucumbers, cauliflower, spinach, onions, carrots, kale, broccoli, brussels-sprouts, etc.

Legumes: peas, chickpeas, beans, peanuts, etc.

Fruit: melons, oranges, bananas, apples, grapes, strawberries, figs, dates, peaches, etc.

Fish and seafood: clams, crabs, salmon, trout, shrimp, tuna, sardines, mackerel, oysters, mussels and more.

Whole grains: corn, barley, brown rice, whole wheat, whole oats, whole grain bread, rye, and pasta.

Yogurt (especially Greek Yogurt) and cheese;

Healthy oil such as avocado oil or olive oil.

Poultry and eggs: duck, chicken, turkey, duck eggs, and quail;

Herbs and spices: rosemary, mint, garlic, basil, sage, pepper, cinnamon, etc.

Nuts and seeds: walnuts, hazelnuts, almonds, pumpkin seeds, cashews, macadamia nuts, sunflower seeds, etc.

Note: all the must eat food items have an abundance of proteins, nutrients, and water.

Fruit salad

Ingredients

1. 1 apple
2. 1 handful of blueberries
3. 1 handful of raspberries
4. ⅛ medium watermelon
5. 1 grapefruit or orange
6. ½ lime

Directions

1. Cut the apple, watermelon, and orange/grapefruit into 1 inch squares.
2. Add to your bowl, along with the berries and squeeze the lime over the fruit.
3. Serve immediately.

You can enjoy whatever fruit is seasonally available.
To create depth and texture, try adding a sprinkle of cinnamon or handful of chopped nuts to your fruit for a zingy way to start your day.

Sardines on Toast

Ingredients

1. 4 slices wholemeal bread
2. 1 teaspoon olive oil
3. 1 tin of sardines in salt water
4. 1 tomato
5. Salt
6. Pepper

Directions

1. Dice the tomato, and add to a bowl with a pinch of salt, pepper and the olive oil. Mix well.
2. Lightly toast the bread, then arrange on a baking tray.
3. Open the tin of sardines and drain the water well. If the fillets are whole, cut them in half, and lay on the toasted bread.
4. Top with the tomato mixture and grill for 7-10 minutes

Avocado Baked Eggs

Ingredients

1. 1 large avocado
2. 2 medium eggs
3. 10g Parmesan cheese
4. Salt
5. Cayenne Pepper

Directions

1. Half the avocado and remove the stone.
2. Place both halves into a muffin tray for support.
3. Break an egg into each half of the avocado and sprinkle with salt, then bake in the oven for 10-15 mins at 180.
4. When the eggs are cooked, top with the parmesan cheese and the cayenne pepper.

Frittata

Ingredients

1. 1 handful cherry tomatoes, halved
2. 1 handful mushrooms, roughly chopped
3. 90g feta cheese
4. 100 g spinach, washed and drained
5. Salt
6. Pepper
7. 1 teaspoon Olive Oil
8. Optional: 3 rashers bacon

Directions

1. Heat the olive oil in a small non-stick frying pan.
2. Once the pan is hot, add the mushrooms and cook until soft. Add the spinach, and cook for a further 2 minutes.
3. When the spinach is wilted, add the tomatoes. If using bacon, grill the rashers, and chop into small pieces.
4. Add to the frying pan.
5. Mix the eggs together in a bowl, and add a pinch of salt and pepper, then pour over the vegetable mix in the frying pan.
6. Cook on a medium heat for 10 minutes, and finish under the grill for a further 5 minutes. Cool slightly before serving

Tostadas

Ingredients

1. 4 small tortillas
2. 1 tomato, diced
3. 50g spinach, washed and drained
4. ½ avocado
5. 3 medium eggs
6. 100g cheddar cheese
7. Salt
8. Pepper
9. 1 teaspoon olive oil
10. Optional: Sliced Jalapenos

Directions

1. Sluice the tortillas with some of the olive oil and oven bake according to manufacturer's instructions.
2. Heat the remaining olive oil in a small non stick frying pan, and cook the spinach and tomato over a low heat.
3. Mix the eggs with a pinch of salt and pepper, and add to the frying pan. Gently scramble the mixture.
4. Once the tortillas are cooked, top with the eggs and vegetables, and finely grate the cheese over the top.
5. Serve with slices of avocado

Traditional Moroccan Bread with Honey

Ingredients

1. 500g plain flour
2. ½ sachet active yeast
3. ½ teaspoon sugar
4. 300ml warm water
5. Salt
6. 50 g sesame seeds
7. Optional: Honey for serving

Directions

1. Sieve the flour into a bowl or mixer, and add two pinches of salt.
2. Mix the yeast and sugar with 50 ml of warm water and let sit until it begins to foam.
3. Then add to the flour along with the remaining warm water.
4. Mix until a dough is formed, and then knead for approximately ten minutes, or until the dough is springy and smooth.
5. Seperate the dough into two balls, and flatten on to a baking tray lined with greaseproof paper. Cover with a clean tea towel and leave to rest for ten minutes.
6. Flatted the disks again, they should be roughly an inch thick. Sprinkle with the sesame

seeds, and cover with the tea towel again, this time leave to rest for one hour.

7. Peirce the top of the dough several times, and bake in the oven at 220°C until golden brown all over, about 20 mins.

8. Serve with honey for dipping, spreading or drizzling.

Breakfast bake

Ingredients

1. 2 onions
2. 1 clove garlic, crushed
3. 6 eggs
4. 300g chorizo
5. 1 red pepper
6. 1 green pepper
7. 2 teaspoons olive oil
8. 1 teaspoon chilli flakes
9. 150g cheddar cheese
10. Salt
11. Pepper

Directions

1. Roughly chop the onions and fry in a non stick pan using half the olive oil, until soft.
2. Chop the chorizo into small cubes, and add to the pan, along with the garlic and chilli flakes.
3. Core and de-seed the peppers, then slice lengthways. Add to the pan and cook the mixture for 7 minutes.
4. Take a small ovenproof dish and grease the bottom and sides using the remaining olive oil.

5. Transfer the contents of the frying pan into the dish. In a bowl, whisk the eggs, and add a pinch of salt and pepper.
6. Then pour over the chorizo and vegetable mix.
7. Grate the cheddar cheese and sprinkle over the top.
8. Oven bake at 180°c for 30 minutes. Cool slightly before serving.

Sweet potato hash with kale

Ingredients

1. 1 large or two medium sweet potatoes
2. 1 onion
3. 3 cloves of garlic, crushed
4. 2 tsps olive oil
5. 500 g curly kale, washed
6. 300g sausage
7. Salt
8. Pepper

Directions

1. Peel the sweet potato and chop into small bite sized chunks.
2. Heat the olive oil in a medium non stick frying pan and cook the cubes of sweet potato for 10-15 mins, until slightly soft.
3. Roughly dice the onion and add to the pan, along with the kale, garlic, salt and pepper.
4. Stir the contents together, and leave to cook on a low heat, until the kale is wilted.
5. Serve with poached eggs.

Scrambled eggs with feta and spinach

Ingredients

1. 4 medium eggs
2. 20ml milk
3. 90g feta
4. 2 handfuls spinach, washed and drained
5. 1 tsp olive oil
6. Salt
7. Cayenne pepper
8. slices wholemeal bread

Directions

1. Whisk the eggs with the milk, and add a pinch of salt and cayenne pepper.
2. Heat the olive oil in a medium non stick frying pan, and add the eggs.
3. Once the eggs start to form, scramble with a wooden spoon.
4. Add the spinach, and crumble the feta.
5. Cook for another 3 minutes, and then serve on toasted wholemeal bread

Zucchini and Goat Cheese Frittata

(Takes 40-50 minutes to prepare | renders 4 servings)

Ingredients

1. 2 medium zucchinis
2. 8 eggs
3. tablespoons milk
4. 1/4 teaspoon salt
5. 1/8 teaspoon pepper
6. 1 tablespoon olive oil
7. 1 clove garlic, crushed
8. 2 ounces goat cheese, crumbled

Directions

This will be a favorite with Zucchini lovers: Begin with preheating the oven to 350 degrees.
1. Slice the zucchinis into rounds of ¼-inch thick;
2. Using a large bowl, whisk the eggs. Add some milk, salt and pepper.
3. In a skillet, preferably a heavy, cast iron one, heat the olive oil while maintaining a medium heat;
4. Add some garlic, and stir for 30 seconds maximum.
5. Add the zucchini rounds and cook for 5 minutes.

6. Add the whisked eggs and stir for 1 minute.
7. Top with cheese and place in the pre-heated oven. Bake for 10-12 minutes. Remove when the eggs are set and leave for 3 minutes.
8. Divide into 4 portions and serve hot.

Savory Fava Beans With Warm Pita Bread

(Takes 10-15 minutes to prepare | renders 4 servings)

Ingredients
1. 1-1/2 tablespoons olive oil
2. 1 large onion, chopped
3. 1 large tomato, diced
4. 1 clove garlic, crushed
5. One 15-ounce can fava beans, undrained
6. 1 teaspoon ground cumin
7. 1/4 cup chopped fresh parsley
8. 1/4 cup lemon juice
9. Salt and pepper to taste
10. Crushed red pepper flakes, to taste
11. 4 whole-grain pita bread pockets

Directions

1. Using a large nonstick skillet, bring the olive oil to medium heat; About 30 seconds should do;
2. Add the onion, garlic and tomato, and sauté for 3 minutes to achieve the so state. Add the fava beans, including liquid and boil it.
3. Maintain medium heat while adding the cumin, parsley and lemon

juice, then add salt, pepper and ground red pepper to taste.

4. Cook on medium heat for 5 minutes heating the Pita in a skillet using medium heat until it is warm. (For about 1 or 2 minutes);

5. Add the warm fava beans mixture to the Pita and serve;

Tuscan Chicken Skillet

Takes 45 Minutes to prepare | renders 4 servings)

Ingredients
1. 1 pound chicken breast tenderloins
2. 1 teaspoon kosher salt
3. 1 teaspoon freshly ground black pepper
4. 2 tablespoons olive oil, divided
5. 12 ounces brown mushrooms, sliced
6. 1/2 cup diced yellow onion
7. 3 cloves garlic, minced
8. 2/3 cup sun-dried tomatoes, chopped
9. 1 teaspoon oregano
10. 1/2 teaspoon thyme
11. 1 (14.5 oz.) can Cannellini Beans, drained and rinsed
12. 2 (14.5 oz.) cans fire roasted diced tomatoes
13. 1 tablespoon sugar
14. Salt and pepper, to taste
15. Parsley for garnish

Directions

1. Heat up a 12-inch large skillet over a medium heat. Even out the thickness of the meat by pounding the thicker parts of the chicken with a meat mallet;
2. Use paper towels for drying the damp chicken, then apply salt and pepper on both sides of the chicken. Add oil to the skillet and then add the chicken;
3. A minimum cooking time of 5 to 6 minutes is required per side of chicken, else cook until the center reaches a temperature of 165 degrees. The temperature can be measured with an instant thermometer;
4. Transfer the cooked chicken to a plate;
5. Reduce the temperature, and place a half tablespoon of butter in the skillet. Add sage and garlic, and sauté until the garlic turns golden brown (this would take nearly 30 seconds at medium temperature;
6. Pour off the chicken broth, then clear out all the browned bits from the pan. You may add more butter according to taste. do remember to stir well after adding butter to allow butter to melt down completely;

7. Serve warm, accompanied by a beverage of your choice.

Barley and Roasted Tomato Risotto

Takes 1 Hour, 10 Minutes to prepare | renders 8 servings)

Ingredients
1. 10 large plum (Roma) tomatoes, about 2 pounds in weight, peeled and quartered;
2. 2 tablespoons extra-virgin olive oil
3. 1 teaspoon salt
4. 1/2 teaspoon freshly ground black pepper
5. 4 cups vegetable stock or broth
6. 3 cups water
7. 2 shallots, chopped
8. 1/4 cup dry white wine, optional
9. 2 cups pearl barley
10. 3 tablespoons chopped fresh basil, plus a few whole leaves for garnish
11. 3 tablespoons chopped fresh flat-leaf (Italian) parsley
12. 1 1/2 tablespoons chopped fresh thyme

13. 1/2 cup grated Parmesan cheese, plus some extra Parmesan, not grated, to fashion curls for garnish

Directions

1. Preheat the oven to 450-degree Fahrenheit
2. Arrange the tomatoes on the baking pan or sheet individually, then drizzle one tablespoon of olive oil onto it.
3. Sprinkle a quarter tablespoon of pepper and salt mix over it. Toss it in to properly mix it. Roast until the tomatoes become so and start changing color to brown after about 25 to 30 minutes;
4. In a large saucepan, add a tablespoon of olive oil, then heat at medium temperature. Add chopped shallots and sauté for about 2 to 3 minutes, until they become translucent and so;
5. You may also add white wine and cook the shallots until most of the liquid evaporates;
6. Add barley and ½ cup of stock mixture, then cook until most of the liquid evaporates. Repeat this process until barley is tender.
7. Fold mixture into tomatoes, then mix in chopped basil, grated cheese, parsley, and thyme.

Mediterranean-Style Grilled Salmon

Takes 25 Minutes to prepare | renders 4 servings)

Ingredients
1. 4 tablespoons chopped fresh basil
2. 1 tablespoon chopped fresh parsley
3. 1 tablespoon minced garlic
4. 2 tablespoons lemon juice
5. 4 salmon fillets, each about 5 ounces
6. Cracked black pepper, to taste
7. 4 green olives, chopped
8. 4 thin slices of lemon

Directions

1. Preheat the grill to medium-high
2. Sprinkle all necessary ingredients on the salmon, then spread a small amount of lemon onto the fillet and add olive oil
3. Rub evenly for proper distribution of the ingredients
4. Place the lemon wedges onto the grill
5. Place the seasoned salmon on the grill and cook at medium heat. Cooking will take about 6 to 8 minutes until done. Remember to flip the salmon over to cook on both sides.

6. Serve directly from the grill with preferred salad

Polenta With Roasted Mediterranean Vegetables

Takes 1 Hour to prepare | renders 6 servings)

Ingredients
1. 1 small eggplant, peeled, cut into 1/4-inch slices
2. 1 small yellow zucchini, cut into 1/4-inch slices
3. 1 small green zucchini, cut into 1/4-inch slices
4. 6 medium mushrooms, sliced
5. 1 sweet red pepper, seeded, cored and cut into chunks
6. 2 tablespoons plus 1 teaspoon extra-virgin olive oil
7. 6 cups water
8. 1 1/2 cups coarse polenta (corn grits)
9. 2 teaspoons trans-free margarine
10. 1/4 teaspoon cracked black pepper
11. 10 ounces frozen spinach, thawed
12. 2 plum (Roma) tomatoes, sliced
13. 6 dry-packed sun-dried tomatoes, soaked in water to rehydrate, drained and chopped
14. 10 ripe olives, chopped
15. 2 teaspoons oregano

Directions

1. Heat the grill and put the racks on the grill about 4 inches above the heat source
2. Place the zucchini, mushrooms, and eggplant on a baking sheet and cook it under low heat. Turn and brush with olive oil when necessary. When it turns brown, remove from the grill. It can be consumed immediately or covered and preserved in the refrigerator.
3. Preheat the oven to 350 Fahrenheit. Heat the water in a saucepan.
4. When the water boils, gradually add polenta. Stir and cook for five minutes. Add a ⅛ teaspoon of black pepper.
5. Spread the polenta on a baking dish and bake for about 10 minutes. When done, cut into 6 wedges and serve with roasted vegetables and oregano.

Vegetable and Garlic Calzone

Takes 60 Minutes to prepare | renders 4 servings)

Ingredients
1. 2 tablespoons olive oil
2. 1 medium onion, chopped
3. 1 clove garlic, minced
4. Pinch of crushed red pepper, optional
5. 1 1/2 cups broccoli florets, cut into small pieces
6. 1 tightly packed cup baby spinach, chopped
7. 1 cup ricotta
8. 1 cup shredded low-fat mozzarella
9. 2 tablespoons grated Parmesan
10. Salt and pepper
11. 1 pound store-bought pizza dough, divided into 4 portions
12. 1 large egg

Directions

1. Preheat the oven to 450 degrees Fahrenheit and then prepare a large baking sheet with waxed paper.
2. Heat the oil in a large skillet. Add onion and sauté for about 10 minutes. Add red pepper and garlic, then sauté for another 30 seconds

3. Lower the heat, then add broccoli and sauté for another two minutes. Place in pre-heated oven and cook until the broccoli becomes crisp and tender.

4. Place parmesan, ricotta, and mozzarella in a bowl and mix with water and salt. Roll out the dough, using flour to prevent sticking. Divide the filling into four portions and place on the dough circles. Fold over the dough to form calzones and seal with a little water r egg white

5. Place calzones onto a baking tray and cut vents into the top of each calzone. Bake until golden (about 15 minutes).

Bean Salad with Balsamic Vinaigrette

Takes 60 Minutes to prepare | renders 6 servings)

Ingredients

Vinaigrette
1. 3 tablespoons balsamic vinegar
2. 3 tablespoons extra-virgin olive oil
3. 1 tablespoon finely chopped fresh basil or 1/2 teaspoon dried basil
4. 4 cloves garlic, minced
5. 1 teaspoon Dijon mustard
6. 1 teaspoon light brown sugar
7. 1/4 teaspoon pepper, or to taste
8. 1/8 teaspoon salt, or to taste
9. 3 cups canned beans, drained and rinsed (such as black beans, garbanzo beans and, kidney beans)
10. 1/2 cup thinly sliced red onion
11. 1/2 cup coarsely chopped green bell pepper
12. 1/2 cup coarsely chopped red bell pepper
13. 2 tablespoons coarsely chopped fresh flat-leaf parsle

Directions

1. Mix all the ingredients for vinaigrette in a medium-sized bowl. Blend well.
2. In a large bowl, mix onion and beans, and gently pour the vinaigrette over the salad mixture.
3. You may enhance the taste by sprinkling pepper and salt over the salad.
4. The salad can be prepared a day before, covered and preserved in a refrigerator.
5. Remember to let the salad warm to room temperature before serving. It can be served on a lettuce leaf placed on each plate.

Braised Kale With Cherry Tomatoes

Takes 35 Minutes to prepare | renders 6 servings)

Ingredients
1. 2 teaspoons extra-virgin olive oil
2. 4 garlic cloves, thinly sliced
3. 1 pound kale (tough stems removed and leaves coarsely chopped)
4. 1/2 cup low-sodium vegetable stock or broth
5. 1 cup cherry tomatoes, halved
6. 1 tablespoon fresh lemon juice
7. 1/4 teaspoon salt
8. 1/8 teaspoon freshly ground black pepper

Directions

1. Place olive oil in a large frying pan and heat over medium heat.
2. Add garlic and sauté until l golden brown (about 1to 2 minutes). Stir in the vegetable stock and kale.
3. Cover the pan, then reduce the heat from medium to low. Cook for

about 5 minutes until the liquid has evaporated and kale appears wilted.

4. Add tomatoes and stir well; cook uncovered until the kale is tender. Remove from the heat, then stir in the lemon juice, pepper, and salt.

5. For best taste, serve hot with suitable beverages.

Roasted Red Pepper With Feta Salad

Takes 45 Minutes to prepare | renders 4-6 servings)

Ingredients

1. 4 bell peppers – red, yellow, and/or orange
2. 1/4 cup olive oil
3. 1/2 small red onion, diced (about 1/2 cup)
4. Handful fresh parsley, chopped (about 1/4 cup chopped)
5. 4 ounces crumbled feta cheese (about 3/4 cup)
6. 1 teaspoon lemon zest

Directions

1. Clean the broiler and pre-heat to 375 degrees.
2. Prepare peppers and put them in a baking dish.
3. Put some olive oil over the peppers and roast for about 35 minutes until wilted and turning brown.
4. Remove peppers from broiler and wrap with foil or a napkin.
5. Allow to cool for at least 30 minutes.

6. Delicately remove as much peel possible. Some bits of peel may be stubborn, so you may leave it.
7. Add lemon zest, parsley, feta and the oil that the peppers baked in. After a few minutes, toss and serve.
8. The salad can be kept in the refrigerator for approximately two days. Remember to let it warm to room temperature before serving.

Grilled Chicken + Dill Greek Yogurt Sauce

Takes 40-60 minutes to prepare | Renders 8 servings)

Ingredients

For the sauce
1. 1 garlic clove, minced
2. 1 cup chopped fresh dill fronds (no stems)
3. 1-1/4 cups whole milk Greek yogurt
4. 1 tablespoon olive oil
5. Juice of ½ lemon or lime
6. Pinch of cayenne pepper, optional
7. Kosher salt, to taste

For the chicken
1. 10 garlic cloves, minced
2. ½ teaspoon paprika
3. ½ teaspoon allspice
4. ½ teaspoon ground nutmeg
5. ¼ teaspoon ground cardamom
6. Kosher salt and freshly ground black pepper
7. 5 tablespoons olive oil, divided
8. 8 boneless, skinless chicken thighs
9. 1 medium red onion, sliced
10. Juice of 1 to 2 lemons
11. Fresh dill fronds, for garnish

Directions

1. Prepare the sauce first: combine the garlic, dill, yogurt, olive oil, cayenne pepper and lime juice in a food processor.
2. Blend until you have a mixture with a smooth and thick consistency.
3. Add some salt for taste, and place in the refrigerator. Chill for at least one hour while you prepare the chicken.and go ahead with the chicken preparation. Until it is ready to use.
4. Mix the garlic, paprika, allspice, nutmeg, cardamom, kosher salt black pepper and 3tablespoons of olive oil in a small bowl. Wipe excess moisture from the chicken thighs.
5. Spread the garlic-spice mixture evenly on the bottom of a casserole dish and place red onion slices on top of the mixture. Place the chicken thighs on top of the onion slices.
6. Add some lemon juice and the remaining olive oil. and toss a bit, if you wish. Keep in the fridge for 2-4 hours.
7. As a finishing touch, heat the grill to medium heat and scrape clean, the grates.
8. Grill the chicken for 5-6 minutes per side. Garnish with fresh dill fronds and serve it with the sauce.

Kale and Feta One-Pot Pasta

Takes 30-40 minutes to prepare | renders 6 servings)

Ingredients

1. 3 tablespoons olive oil
2. 6 to 8 cups solidly packed fresh kale leaves
3. 1/8 teaspoon salt
4. 4-1/2 cups water
5. 1 pint cherry tomatoes, halved
6. 1 package (8-ounces) Fettuccini Pasta
7. 3 garlic cloves, minced
8. salt and fresh ground pepper to taste
9. 2 tablespoons Extra Virgin Olive Oil
10. 1/2-cup crumbled feta cheese

Directions

1. Heat the olive oil, preferably in a stockpot.
2. Add kale leaves and salt and cook over medium heat.
3. Stir for 2 minutes.
4. Remove from heat and add some water.
5. Add halved tomatoes, garlic, pasta, pepper and salt.

6. Keep the heat high and bring to boil.
7. Tone down the heat and leave to cook for the next 15 minutes. Once the pasta is completely cooked, remove and let it stand for 2 minutes.
8. Add some extra virgin olive oil and stir in crumbled feta cheese.Serve hot.

Mediterranean Tacos

20-30 minutes of preparation | 4 servings)

Ingredients
1. 2 tomatoes, diced
2. 1 large cucumber, peeled and diced
3. 1 small red onion, diced
4. 2 tablespoons red wine vinegar
5. 1 tablespoon Extra Virgin Olive Oil
6. 1/2 teaspoon Whole Spice Himalayan Pink Sea Salt
7. 1/2 teaspoon pepper
8. 1 container hummus
9. 2 chicken breasts, cooked and sliced (or store bought rotisserie chicken)
10. 1 1/2 cups shredded lettuce
11. 1 can artichoke hearts, drained sliced black olives
12. 1/2 cup feta cheese, crumbled
13. 4 pita breads

Directions

1. Place tomatoes, cucumber, Extra Virgin Olive Oil, red wine vinegar, red onion, pepper and Himalayan pink sea salt In a large bowl
2. Toss the to get a fine blend and set to the side.
3. Warm the pita bread.
4. Spread hummus, to taste, inn the bottom of each pita bread.
5. Add some cooked chicken, lettuce, artichoke hearts, tomato salad, olives and feta cheese.
6. Enjoy the taco.

Skinny Bruschetta Chicken

Takes 30-40 minutes to prepare | renders 4 servings)

Ingredients

1. 3 medium vine-ripened tomatoes
2. 2 small cloves garlic, minced
3. 1/4 cup chopped red onion
4. 2 tbsp fresh basil leaves, chopped
5. 1 tbsp extra virgin oil
6. 1 tbsp balsamic vinegar
7. kosher salt and fresh cracked pepper to taste
8. 3 oz low fat mozzarella, diced (omit for whole30, paleo)
9. 1.25 lbs 8 (thinly sliced) chicken cutlets

Directions

1. Mix the olive oil, onions, ¼ tbsp kosher salt and pepper with some balsamic vinegar. Set aside for a few minutes.
2. Chop the tomatoes and place in a large bowl. Combine this with the olive oil mixture. Add salt and pepper to taste. Leave to stand for at least for at least 10-minutes.

3. Preheat the grill to a medium temperature. Ensure the grates are clean and oiled to ensure that the chicken doesn't stick.

4. Place chicken on grill, and grill until lightly browned, and set aside on a platter.

5. Toss in some of the earlier prepared mixture and some cheese, and serve.

Mediterranean Greek Salad

Takes 10-15 minutes to prepare | renders 2 servings)

Ingredients

1. 3 tablespoons extra virgin olive oil
2. 1½ tablespoons lemon juice
3. 1 clove garlic—minced
4. ½ teaspoon dried oregano
5. ¼ teaspoon sea salt
6. ¼ teaspoon freshly ground black pepper, plus extra for garnish
7. 3 tomatoes, cut into wedges
8. ¼ red onion, sliced into rings
9. ½ cucumber, sliced into thick half-moons
10. ½ green pepper (capsicum), julienned
11. 4 oz (120g) feta cheese, cut into small cubes
12. 16 kalamata olives

Directions

1. Place the olive oil, garlic, oregano, lime juice, salt and pepper in a small jar.
2. Make sure the jar has a screw-top lid to shake and combine.
3. Close the jar. Shake and combine.

4. Place the salad and its ingredients in a large bowl.

5. Pour the prepared mixture over the salad and toss until it gels together.

6. Garnish the salad with some black pepper to taste, then serve.

Penne with Shrimp

Takes 30 minutes to prepare | renders 4-6 servings)

Ingredients

1. 1 pound penne pasta
2. 1/4 cup olive oil
3. 1 pound medium shrimp, peeled
4. 4 cloves garlic, minced
5. 1/2 teaspoon kosher salt, plus extra for seasoning
6. 1/2 teaspoon freshly ground black pepper, plus extra for seasoning
7. 1 (15-ounce) can whole tomatoes, drained, roughly chopped
8. 1/2 cup chopped fresh basil leaves
9. 1/2 cup chopped fresh flat-leaf parsley
10. 1/4 teaspoon crushed red pepper flakes
11. 1 cup white wine
12. 1/3 cup clam juice
13. 3/4 cup heavy whipping cream
14. 1/2 cup grated Parmesan

Directions

1. Boil a large pot of salted water on high heat. Add the pasta and cook until tender. Stir for about 8-10 minutes.
2. Drain the pasta and keep it aside.
3. Heat the oil in a large skillet over medium heat. Add the shrimp, garlic, 1/2 teaspoon of salt, and 1/2 teaspoon of pepper.
4. Stir frequently until the shrimp is cooked; it can take up to 3 minutes. Remove the shrimp and keep aside.
5. Add tomatoes, including some red pepper flakes, followed by 1/4 cup basil and 1/4 cup parsley. Cook for around 2 minutes.
6. Add wine, clam juice, and heavy cream and reduce heat to low. Simmer for 7-8 minutes.
7. Add 1/4 cup of the Parmesan, the cooked shrimp, the cooked pasta, and the remaining herbs.
8. Toss well and season with salt and pepper.

Avocado Egg Salad

Takes 15-20 minutes to prepare | renders 2 servings

Ingredients

1. 1 medium avocado, piped and peeled
2. 2 tablespoons light mayonnaise or Greek yogurt
3. 1 1/2 teaspoons fresh lemon juice
4. 4 hard-boiled eggs, peeled and chopped
5. 1 medium-length celery stalk, finely chopped (about 3 tablespoons)
6. 1 tablespoon finely chopped chives, parsley or dill
7. Salt and fresh ground black pepper to taste

Directions

1. To boil the eggs: place in a saucepan and cover with cold water; place the lid on the saucepan and boil for 12 minutes. Remove the eggs from the hot water and place in cold water to crack the shells.
2. Slice the eggs into rounds.
3. Mash the avocado well with some mayonnaise and lemon juice in a

medium-sized bowl. Add the eggs, celery and chives.

4. Str the mixture well, season it with salt and pepper to taste, and serve.

Garlic Mushroom Kebabs

Takes 30-35 minutes to prepare | renders 2 servings)

Ingredients

1. 1/4 cup balsamic vinegar
2. 2 tablespoons olive oil
3. 3 cloves garlic, pressed
4. 1/2 teaspoon dried oregano
5. 1/2 teaspoon dried basil
6. Kosher salt and freshly ground black pepper to taste
7. 1 pound cremini mushrooms
8. 2 tablespoons chopped fresh parsley leaves

Directions

1. Pre-heat the oven to 425-degree F. Add some oil on a baking sheet, or coat it with a non-stick spray.
2. In a large bowl, add together some balsamic vinegar, olive oil, garlic, oregano and basil, salt and pepper.
3. Stir in the mushrooms and let it stand for 10-15 minutes.
4. Impale the mushrooms with skewers and place on the greased baking

sheet. Place into the pre-heated oven and roast for 15-20 minutes.

5. Garnish with parsley and serve..

Mediterranean Salmon

Takes 20-25 minutes to prepare | renders 2 servings

Ingredients

1. 2 salmon filets; 2 cup mixed olives
2. 1/2 cup diced tomato
3. 1/3 cup feta crumbles
4. 1 tablespoon finely chopped Italian parsley
5. splash of olive oil
6. splash of balsamic vinegar
7. sea salt and pepper to taste

Directions

1. Pre-heat the oven to 350-degrees.
2. Remove the skin from the rinsed salmon and sprinkle some sea salt and black pepper on the top.
3. Place the salmon in the baking dish and add some water.
4. Place in pre-heated oven and bake it for 15 minutes.
5. Top with feta-olive tapenade.
6. To make Tapenade: chop the tomatoes and olives in small dices, including the Italian parsley.

7. Mix all of these with the feta crumbles and add more olive oil and balsamic vinegar.

8. Add some sea salt and pepper for taste, and serve.

Warm Olives with Rosemary

Takes 30-35 minutes to prepare | renders 2 servings)

Ingredients

1. 2 tablespoons extra virgin olive oil
2. 2 garlic cloves, thinly sliced
3. Zested rind of 1 orange
4. 2 rosemary sprigs
5. 2 thyme sprigs
6. 2 fresh bay leaves
7. 1 tablespoon coriander seeds
8. 1 teaspoon fennel seeds
9. 300g good-quality mixed olives

Description

1. Heat the following ingredients together in a pan: olive oil, garlic, zest, rosemary, thyme, bay leaves, coriander seeds and fennel seeds. Keep the heat low and take it down after approximately 3 minutes.
2. Add the olives and toss gently.
3. Cook for around 1-2 minutes until warm.
4. Serve hot with an aperitif.

Mediterranean Grilled Vegetable Tagine

Takes 40-55 minutes to prepare | renders 4-6 servings)

Ingredients

1. 1/4 cup extra virgin olive oil
2. 2 medium yellow onions, peeled and chopped
3. 8-10 garlic cloves, peeled and chopped
4. 2 large carrots, peeled and chopped
5. 2 large russet potatoes, peeled and cubed
6. 1 large sweet potato, peeled and cubed
7. Salt to taste
8. 1 tbsp Harissa spice blend
9. 1 tsp ground coriander
10. 1 tsp ground cinnamon
11. 1/2 tsp ground turmeric
12. 2 cups canned whole peeled tomatoes
13. 1/2 cup chopped dried apricot
14. 1 quart low-sodium vegetable broth (or broth of your choice)
15. 2 cups cooked chickpeas
16. Juice of 1 lemon
17. Handful fresh parsley leaves

Directions

1. In a large pot, heat the olive oil over
2. Add some onions and keep the heat between medium and high. Sauté for 5 minutes while tossing.
3. Add some garlic and include all the chopped veggies. Add some salt and spices and toss .
4. After cooking for 5-7 minutes, add some tomatoes, apricot, broth and a pinch of salt. Cook for 5-10 minutes over medium heat.
5. Reduce the heat, cover and let it stand for 25 minutes.
6. Stir in the chickpeas and simmer for 5 minutes on low heat.
7. Add the lime juice and fresh parsley.
8. Add some salt and extra virgin oil and serve.

Zucchini Noodles With Poached Egg Topper

Takes 30-35 minutes to prepare | renders 4 servings)

Ingredients

1. 2 tbsp. extra virgin olive oil
2. 2 medium garlic cloves, minced
3. 1/2 tsp. red chili flakes
4. 4 medium zucchini, spiralized into noodles
5. 1/4 tsp. each salt and pepper
6. 2 cups halved cherry tomatoes
7. 2 cups tightly packed baby spinach
8. 1 tsp. lemon zest
9. 1 tbsp. fresh lemon juice
10. 4 large EGGS
11. 1/4 cup shaved Parmesan
12. 1/4 cup thinly sliced basil leaves

Directions

1. Heat the oil in a large skillet over medium heat. Add garlic and chilli flakes and cook until soft.
2. Add zucchini noodles along with salt and pepper and toss gently for 2 minutes.

3. Stir in the tomatoes, spinach and lemon zest (including juice) and cook for 2 minutes.
4. Add some water, bring to the boil.
5. Slip the eggs into water, holding dish.
6. Cook for 3-5 minutes without stirring.
7. Remove the eggs with a slotted spoon and drain well.
8. Serve the dish

African Heritage Mango & Papaya After-Chop

Takes 30-35 minutes to prepare | renders 2 servings)

Ingredients

1. ¼ of a papaya or 1 peach, chopped into cubes
2. 1 mango, skin peeled and chopped into cubes
3. 1 tablespoon coconut milk
4. ½ teaspoon honey or maple syrup
5. 1 tablespoon chopped peanuts

Directions

1. Cut the papaya open and scoop out the black seeds.
2. Peel the papaya.
3. Chop into cubes.
4. Peel the mango and slice the fruit from the pit. Chop the chunks into small cubes.
5. Place the fruit in a bowl and add in some coconut milk, honey, and peanuts over the fruit. Stir.
6. Serve immediately, or keep in the fridge and enjoy it over the next 2 days.

Creamy Mediterranean Paninis

Takes 25 minutes to prepare | renders 4 servings)

Ingredients

1. 1/2 cup Hellmann's® or Best Foods® Mayonnaise Dressing with Olive Oil, divided
2. 1/4 cup chopped fresh basil leaves
3. 2 tablespoons finely chopped oil-cured black olives
4. 8 slices whole grain bread (about 1/2-inch thick)
5. 1 small zucchini, thinly sliced
6. 4 slices provolone cheese
7. 1 jar (7 oz.) roasted red peppers, drained and sliced

Directions

1. Place the basil, ¼ cup of Mayonnaise, some olive oil and some olives in a small bowl.
2. Spread the mixture on the bread slices, then layer the bread into 4 slices with a bit of zucchini, provolone, peppers and bacon on top. Combine the bread slices.

3. Spread the rest of the Mayonnaise (¼ cup), on the outer part of the sandwiches and cook in a big skillet or a grill pan. Choose medium heat. After the sandwiches have turned golden brown, add some cheese and let it melt. Serve the dish.

Mediterranean Skewers with Bloody Mary Vinaigrette

Takes 30-35 minutes to prepare | renders 32 servings)

Ingredients
1. 1/2 cup tomato juice
2. 2 tablespoons premium vodka
3. 1/8 teaspoon Worcestershire sauce
4. 2 celery hearts, finely diced (about 3 tablespoons)
5. 1/4 teaspoon kosher salt
6. 1/4 teaspoon freshly ground black pepper
7. Bocconcini, grape tomatoes, artichoke hearts, and kalamata olives (about 32 each)
8. 1/8 teaspoon hot sauce
9. 1/4 teaspoon prepared horseradish
10. 2 tablespoons extra-virgin olive oil

Directions

We do not always have the time to prepare lavish dishes. For those moments when we need to be quick without compromising on the taste, make the easiest dish:
1. Mix some tomato juice, hot sauce, horseradish, oil, vodka,

Worcestershire Sauce, celery, salt, and pepper in a medium-sized bowl. Keep it in the refrigerator.

2. Thread a bocconcini ball, tomato, olive, and artichoke heart onto each skewer.

3. Serve with vinaigrette.

Vegetable Omelet

Takes 30-40 minutes to prepare | renders 4 servings

Ingredients
1. 1 tablespoon olive oil
2. 2 cups thinly sliced fresh fennel bulb
3. 1 Roma tomato, diced
4. 1/4 cup piped green brine-cured olives, chopped
5. 1/4 cup artichoke hearts, marinated in water, rinsed, drained, and chopped
6. 6 eggs
7. 1/4 teaspoon salt
8. 1/2 teaspoon black pepper
9. 1/2 cup goat cheese, crumbled
10. 2 tablespoons chopped fresh dill, basil, or parsley

Directions

You can start preparing this Mediterranean breakfast by preheating the oven to 325 degrees. While waiting for the oven, do the following:

1. Using large skillet, heat the olive oil to medium temperature.
2. Add the fennel, and sauté for around 5 minutes until soft

3   Add some tomatoes, olives and artichoke hearts and sauté for around 3 minutes until soft.
4   Whisk the eggs in a separate bowl, then sprinkle over some salt and pepper;
5   Pour the whisked eggs into the large skillet and stir in with the olives and tomatoes, using a heat-proof spoon;
6   After stirring for two-minutes cover the omelet with cheese and place in the pre-heated oven. Bake for around 5 minutes. Make sure that he eggs are well-cooked;
7   Top with dill, basil, or parsley.
8   Remove the omelet from the skillet and cut into four wedges

Lemon Scones

(Takes 30-40 minutes to prepare | renders 12 servings)

Dedicated to those of us who wish to have a healthy lemon-flavored breakfast.

Ingredients
1. 2 cups (plus an additional 1/4 cup) flour
2. 2 tablespoons sugar
3. 1/2 teaspoon baking soda
4. 1/2 teaspoon salt
5. 1/4 cup butter
6. Zest of 1 lemon
7. 3/4 cup reduced-fat buttermilk
8. 1 cup powdered sugar
9. 1 to 2 teaspoons lemon juice

Directions
1. Pre-heat the oven to 400-degrees. Place sugar, salt, baking soda and 2 cups of flour in a medium bowl;
2. Use a pastry blender or a food processor to cut in the butter until the mixture looks like fine bread crumbs;
3. Add the lemon zest and buttermilk and stir well;
4. Add the remaining flour and turn the dough out. Gently knead the mixture

six times. . Shape into a ball, then flatten to a circle, preferably ½-inch thick;

5.   Cut the circle into 4 wedges, then divide each wedge into 3 smaller wedges. You will have 12 wedges;
6.   Place the wedges on a greased baking sheet and bake for 12-15 minutes, or until golden brown;
7.   Mix the powdered sugar with just enough lemon juice form a thin frosting. Apply the frosting and serve.
☐

Slow Cooker Mediterranean Beef Stew with Rosemary and Balsamic Vinegar

(Takes 8 Hours, 25 Minutes to prepare| renders 6 servings)

You will need a 2.5 quart Crock-Pot or a 3-1/2-Quart Slow Cooke

Ingredients

1. 1-2 Tablespoons Olive oil (depends on your pan)
2. 8 oz. sliced mushrooms
3. 1 onion, diced in 1/2 inch pieces
4. 2 lbs. trimmed and diced chuck steak, cut in bite-sized pieces (about 2-3 cups meat; for stove-top cooking you may want to use a more tender cut of beef)
5. 1 cup beef stock (use 2 cups for stovetop cooking)
6. 1 can (14.5 oz.) diced tomatoes with juice
7. 1/2 cup tomato sauce
8. 1/4 cup balsamic vinegar, preferably "Fini"
9. 1 can black olives, halved or quartered
10. 1/2 cup garlic cloves, cut in thin slices (optional, but good)

11.   2 Tablespoons finely chopped fresh rosemary, or 1 Tablespoon dried cracked rosemary;

12.   2 Tablespoons finely chopped fresh parsley (or use 1 Tablespoon dried parsley)

13.   1 Tablespoons capers (you can use more)

Directions

1. Heat olive oil in a frying pan over medium heat and then add mushrooms to it. Cook until mushrooms turn brown. Transfer to a slow cooker
2. Cook some diced onions for about 5 minutes using the frying pan, then transfer them to the slow cooker;
3. Cook beef in the frying pan and brown well for about 10 minutes. to the slow cooker
4. Prepare beef stock and add to the slow cooker;
5. Add capers, rosemary, parsley, tomato sauce, olives, balsamic vinegar, garlic and black pepper to the slow cooker and stir it gently for proper mixing.
6. Close the slow cooker and cook for about 6-8 hours on low heat. High heat for 3-4 hours may work, but is not recommended.

☐

Mediterranean Zucchini Sticks

Takes 20 Minutes to prepare | renders 4 servings)

Ingredients
1. 4 zucchinis, medium
2. 1 cup red bell pepper, finely chopped
3. 1/2 cup tomatoes, finely chopped
4. 1/2 cup Kalamata olives, finely chopped
5. 3 large garlic cloves, minced
6. 1 tbsp oregano, dried
7. 1/4 tsp ground black pepper
8. 1/4 cup feta cheese, crumbled
9. 1/4 cup parsley, finely chopped

Directions
1. Pre-heat the oven to a temperature of 350-degree Fahrenheit;
2. Cut the zucchini symmetrically lengthwise, then scoop out the middle portion with the help of a melon baller or a spoon;
3. Mix tomato, black pepper, bell pepper, oregano, garlic and olives in a medium-sized bowl. Scoop this mixture into each of the zucchini, making sure that it is distributed evenly

4. After distributing the mixture into the zucchini, place the zucchini on a large

baking dish or baking sheet, place in the pre-heated oven and bake for 15 minutes;;.

5. After baking for 15 minutes, top up the dish with cheese and increase the heat to high. Bake until the cheese has browned;

6. Remove from the oven, sprinkle some parsley on it and serve;

Grouper with tomato-olive sauce

Takes 35 Minutes to prepare | renders 4 servings)

Ingredients
1. Cooking spray
2. 1/2 cup chopped onion
3. 2 teaspoons boiled minced garlic
4. 1/2 cup dry white wine
5. 1/3 cup fat-free, less-sodium chicken broth
6. 1 cup quartered cherry tomatoes
7. 1/4 cup piped ripe olives, halved
8. 1 tablespoon chopped fresh herbs, such as basil, parsley, or oregano
9. 1 tablespoon olive oil
10. 4 (6-ounce) grouper fillets (about 1/2-inch thick)
11. 1/4 teaspoon salt
12. 1/4 teaspoon black pepper

Directions
1. Add a quarter teaspoon salt and ⅛ teaspoon pepper in a nonstick frying pan with grouper socks. Also, add one and a half teaspoon of olive oil, then cook over medium heat.
2. Add the pieces of fish on the pan and sear on both sides until light brown.

It would take a few minutes per side. Transfer to a plate.

3. Add another spoon of olive oil and cook onion. Add garlic, followed by jalapeno, capers, olives, capers, and tomatoes. Sauté for about 10 minutes.

4. Mix a quarter teaspoon of salt and an ⅛ teaspoon of pepper together, add to spicy mix then add all of these to the pan of fish. Cook for more or less 6-8 minutes.

5. Serve the grouper steaks warm after stirring the vegetables into lime juice. You may also pour some of the sauce over the grouper steaks.

Mediterranean-Style Grilled Salmon

Takes 35 minutes to prepare | renders 8 servings)

Ingredients

1. 4 tablespoons chopped fresh basil
2. 1 tablespoon chopped fresh parsley
3. 1 tablespoon minced garlic
4. 2 tablespoons lemon juice
5. 4 salmon fillets, each about 5 ounces
6. Cracked black pepper, to taste
7. 4 green olives, chopped
8. 4 thin slices of lemon

Directions

1. Preheat the grill to medium-high
2. Sprinkle all necessary ingredients on the salmon, then spread a small amount of lemon onto the fillet and add olive oil
3. Rub evenly for proper distribution of the ingredients
4. Place the lemon wedges onto the grill
5. Place the seasoned salmon on the grill and cook at medium heat. Cooking will take about 6 to 8 minutes until done.

Remember to flip the salmon over to cook on both sides.
6.   Serve directly from the grill with preferred salad

Artichokes Alla Romana

Takes 40 Minutes to prepare | renders 4 servings)

Ingredients
1. 10 small to medium artichokes, stems included and cleaned and halved; make sure buy the tenderest artichokes available.
2. 2 tablespoons chopped fresh mint (about 5 grams)
3. 2 large cloves of garlic, chopped
4. 2 teaspoons dried oregano (about 1 gram)
5. 3/4 teaspoon salt (about 3 grams)
6. 1/4 cup olive oil (about 55 grams)
7. 1 cup water (about 235 grams)

Directions
1. In a small bowl, mix together the garlic, parsley, salt, mint and one tablespoon of oil.
2. Scoop the mixture into the cavity of the cavities of prepared artichokes
3. After filling each artichoke arrange the the artichokes in a deep pan so that they are close together, in a fixed position. This will ensure proper cooking.
5. Add wine, oil, a pinch of salt and boiling water. Cover the pan and let the artichokes simmer for one hour.
6. Serve the dish at room temperature.

Beet Walnut Salad

Takes 1 Hour, 05 Minutes to prepare | renders 6 servings)

Ingredients

1. 2 bunches baby beetroot, trimmed
2. Olive oil, for greasing
3. 140g (2/3 cup) castor sugar
4. 55g (1/2 cup) walnut halves
5. 1/2 teaspoon sea salt flakes
6. 2 bunches rocket leaves
7. 80g goat's cheese, crumbled
8. 60ml (1/4 cup) extra virgin olive oil
9. 1 tablespoon red wine vinegar

Directions

1. Preheat the oven to 400-degree Fahrenheit.
2. Wrap aluminum foil around each beet and place on the baking sheet.
3. Roast the beet in the oven for about an hour.
4. After roasting, remove the foil from the beet, then peel of the skin. Using plastic gloves is recommended to prevent skin staining.

5. When peeled, chop the beet into large chunks, then place into a medium

sized bowl. Add the rest of the ingredients and let the beet marinate before serving.

6. Serve by arranging the beet chunks on the plate and using parsley and lemon slices to garnish.

Fresh Tomato Crostini

Takes 2-3 hours to prepare | renders 6-8 servings)

Ingredients

1. 2 teaspoons extra-virgin olive oil
2. 4 garlic cloves, thinly sliced
3. 1 pound kale (tough stems removed and leaves coarsely chopped)
4. 1/2 cup low-sodium vegetable stock or broth
5. 1 cup cherry tomatoes, halved
6. 1 tablespoon fresh lemon juice
7. 1/4 teaspoon salt
8. 1/8 teaspoon freshly ground black pepper

Directions

1. Using a large bowl, mix minced garlic and tomatoes together. Season gently with pepper and salt.
2. Add three tablespoons oil and vinegar. Toss well for even distribution.
3. Place in a medium sized saucepan
4. Cover and leave to marinate at room temperature. Occasional stirring may help to develop flavor.
5. Brush one side of toasted bread with sliced side of a garlic clove.

6. Combine basil with tomato mix in a dish and toss properly.
7. Season with salt and pepper to taste. Prepare crostini on a tray. Place tomato mixture on top of each crostini.

Grilled Chicken and Grape Skewers

Takes 30-40 minutes to prepare | renders 4 servings)

Ingredients

1. 2 tablespoons olive oil
2. 1/2 teaspoon lemon zest
3. 1 tablespoon lemon juice
4. 2 cloves garlic, minced
5. 1 teaspoon ground cumin
6. 1/2 teaspoon ground coriander
7. 1/2 teaspoon salt
8. 1 pound boneless skinless chicken breast, cut into 3/4-inch cubes
9. 8 (10-inch) skewers
10. 1 1/2 cups seedless green grapes
11. Cooking spray
12. 2 tablespoons freshly chopped mint leaves
13. 1 lemon, cut into wedges

Directions

1. Prepare a marinade by pouring some oil, lemon zest and lemon juice into a medium sized bowl and adding some cumin, coriander, garlic, and salt.

2. Add the chicken to the marinade. Marinate for around 20 minutes while soaking the wooden skewers in water.
3. Using the skewers, impale 4 grapes and 4 pieces of chicken, alternating them.

4. Medium-heat a grill pan or prepare an outdoor grill.
5. Grill chicken for about 3 to 4 minutes each side. Sprinkle with mint and serve with lemon wedges.

☐

Kale, Cannellini and Farro Stew

Takes 30-40 minutes to prepare | renders 6 servings)

Ingredients

1. 2 Tbsp olive oil
2. 1 cup carrots diced (about 2 medium)
3. 1 cup chopped yellow onion (1 small)
4. 1 cup chopped celery (about 2)
5. 4 cloves garlic , minced
6. 5 cups low-sodium vegetable broth
7. 1 (14.5 oz) can diced tomatoes
8. 1 cup farro , rinsed
9. 1 tsp dried oregano
10. 1 bay leaf
11. Salt to taste
12. 1/2 cup slightly packed parsley sprigs (stems included)
13. 4 cups slightly packed chopped kale , thick ribs removed
14. 1 (15 oz) can cannellini beans, drained and rinsed
15. 1 Tbsp fresh lemon juice
16. Feta cheese, crumbled, for serving

Directions

1. Heat the oil in a large pot over medium heat.
2. Add onions, carrots and celery. Sauté for 3 minutes.
3. Add garlic and sauté for an additional 30 seconds.
4. Add vegetable broth, tomatoes, farro, bay leaves, oregano and salt.
5. Place parsley on top of the mixture and bring to the boil.
6. Cover and let soup boil for 20 minutes
7. Remove the parsley and stir together with kale for 10-15 minutes.
8. Add cannellini beans and continue cooking until both farro and kale are tender.
9. Remove bay leaves and pour in lemon juice, adding some additional vegetables and some water, if desired.
10. Serve soup with warm feta cheese.

☐

Mediterranean Chicken Pasta

Takes 30-45 minutes to prepare | renders 8 servings)

Ingredients

1. 1 package (12 ounces) uncooked tricolor spiral pasta
2. 2 tablespoons olive oil, divided
3. 1 pound boneless skinless chicken breasts, cut into 1/2-inch pieces
4. 1 large sweet red pepper, chopped
5. 1 medium onion, chopped
6. 3 garlic cloves, peeled and thinly sliced
7. 1 cup white wine or reduced-sodium chicken broth
8. 1/4 cup sun-dried tomatoes (not packed in oil)
9. 1 teaspoon dried basil
10. 1 teaspoon Italian seasoning
11. 1/2 teaspoon salt
12. 1/4 teaspoon crushed red pepper flakes
13. 1/4 teaspoon pepper
14. 1 can (14-1/2 ounces) reduced-sodium chicken broth
15. 1 can (14 ounces) water-packed quartered artichoke hearts, drained
16. 1 package (6 ounces) fresh baby spinach

17. 1 cup (4 ounces) crumbled feta cheese
18. Thinly sliced fresh basil leaves and shaved Parmesan cheese, optional

Directions

1. Begin preparations by cooking the pasta. Heat 1 tbsp oil in a stockpot.
2. Add the chicken and stir in for 4-6 minutes. Remove from heat when no pinkish shade remains in chicken.
3. Heat the left-over oil over medium heat. Sprinkle onions with red pepper and stir well for 4-5 minutes.
4. Once the onion becomes tender, add garlic and keep cooking.
5. Add sun-dried tomatoes, wine and seasonings and let it boil.
6. Reduce the heat and keep stirring.
7. Add artichoke hearts and broth, followed by spinach and chicken. Cook until the spinach is wilted.
8. Stir in some feta cheese and preferred toppings and serve.

Mediterranean Tuna Salad with a Zesty Dijon Mustard Vinaigrette

Takes 20-30 minutes to prepare | renders 6-8 servings)

Ingredients

Zesty Dijon Mustard Vinaigrette
1. 2 1/2 tsp good quality Dijon mustard
2. Zest of 1 lime
3. Juice of 1 1/2 limes
4. 1/3 cup extra virgin olive oil
5. 1/2 tsp sumac
6. Pinch of salt and pepper
7. 1/2 tsp crushed red pepper flakes, optional

1. 3 5-ounce cans tuna in olive oil
2. 2 1/2 celery stalks, chopped
3. 1/2 English cucumber, chopped
4. 4-5 whole small radishes, stems removed, chopped
5. 3 green onions, both white and green parts, chopped
6. 1/2 medium-sized red onion, finely chopped
7. 1/2 cup cup piped Kalamata olives, halved

8. 1 bunch of fresh parsley, stems removed, chopped (about 1 cup)
9. 10-15 fresh mint leaves, stems removed, finely chopped (about 1/2 cup)
10. Six slices heirloom tomatoes for serving
11. Pita chips or pita pockets for serving

Directions

Beginning with Zesty Mustard Vinaigrette
1. Mix together in a small bowl: Dijon mustard; lime juice and lime zest.
2. Add some olive oil, salt and pepper and sumac along with some crushed pepper flakes (optional). Keep stirring until the blend is smooth. Keep Vinaigrette aside.
3. Tuna Salad: Add together in a large salad bowl: 3 Tuna; chopped vegetables; kalamata olives; mint leaves and fresh parsley. Mix gently with a spoon.
4. Combine with vinaigrette and mix until the on the tuna pieces are well-covered by vinaigrette. Cover the bowl and keep it the refrigerate for 30 minutes.
5. Toss the salad and serve with sliced tomatoes or pita chips/bread .

Mediterranean Breakfast Quinoa

Takes 20-25 minutes to prepare | renders 4 servings)

Ingredients

1. 1 cup quinoa, rinsed well and drained (any color)
2. 3 cups water
3. ¼ cup walnuts
4. 4 extra large (or 8 smaller) dried figs
5. 8 dried apricot halves
6. 1 teaspoon cinnamon

Directions

1. Boil quinoa in water; keep on low heat, covered, for around 15 minutes.
2. Chop the figs, apricots, and walnuts into tiny pieces.
3. You will know that the quinoa is done when it looks like it has popped open, revealing the germ of the kernel.. All of the liquid will be absorbed.
4.
5. Place the chopped fruits and nuts, the the cinnamon and the quinoa, in a large bowl.
6. Divide the quinoa mixture into 4 portions and add ½ cup of milk to each

portion when set. Cover and keep it in the refrigerator.

Alternatively, you may keep the quinoa preparation in the fridge and add milk when served. .

Easy Mediterranean Fish

30-45 minutes of preparation | 2 servings)

Ingredients

1. 4 (6-ounce) fillets halibut
2. 1 tablespoon Greek seasoning.
3. 1 large tomato, chopped
4. 1 onion, chopped
5. 1 (5-ounce) jar piped kalamata olives
6. 1/4 cup capers
7. 1/4 cup olive oil
8. 1 tablespoon lemon juice
9. Salt and pepper to taste.

Directions

1. Preheat the oven to 350-degrees.
2. Place the halibut fillets on a large aluminium foil sheet and season using Greek seasoning.
3. Mix tomato, onion, olives, capers, olive oil, lemon juice, salt, and pepper together in a bowl.
4. Toss the tomato mixture over the halibut and seal the edges of the foil.
5. Place the sealed package on a baking sheet and place in the preheated oven; Bake for about 30-40 minutes. Served when done.

Sicilian Spaghetti

Takes 45 minutes to prepare | renders 4 servings)

Ingredients

1. 2 aubergines
2. 3 cloves of garlic
3. ½ a bunch of fresh basil , (15g)
4. 1 teaspoon dried oregano
5. 1 teaspoon dried chilli flakes
6. Olive oil
7. 1 tablespoon baby capers
8. 1 tablespoon red wine vinegar
9. 1 x 400 g of quality plum tomatoes
10. 320 g dried whole wheat spaghetti
11. 50 g pecorino cheese
12. extra virgin olive oil

Directions

1. Chop the aubergines into chunks of about 2 cm.
2. Sprinkle with sea salt and set aside for 20 minutes. The salt will draw out the moisture.
3. In a large bowl, mix the garlic slices and basil leaves. Rinse and dry the aubergines and add to the garlic and basil.

4.   Add the oregano, chilli flakes, a splash of olive oil and some sea salt and black pepper. Toss well.
5.   Place some olive oil into a large frying pan and heat to a medium temperature. Add the aubergines in a single layer and fry for 5 to 8 minutes.
6.   Add some olive oil, garlic, capers and basil stalks.
7.   Stir in vinegar and tomatoes.
8.   Cook the spaghetti in a pan of boiling salted water.
9.   When done, drain the spaghetti and add some water to the aubergine sauce, then add the aubergine sauce to the spaghetti.
10.   Add some extra virgin olive oil and cheese, and toss well.
11.   Divide into four servings and add some extra cheese and basil leaves .

Caprese-Style Portobellos

Takes 10-15 minutes to prepare | renders 2 servings)

Ingredients

1. large portobello mushroom caps, gills removed
2. cherry tomatoes, halved
3. shredded or fresh mozzarella (both are okay but the dry shredded version works better to limit moisture.
4. fresh basil
5. olive oil

Directions

1. Pre-heat the oven to 400 degrees.
2. Line your baking sheet with foil to keep cleaning to a minimum.
3. Brush each mushroom cap and olive oil.
4. Slice cherry or grape tomatoes in half. Place in a bowl, spread on some olive oil, and add chopped basil, salt and pepper. Let it steep for a few minutes.
5. Place the cheese on the bottom side of each mushroom cap. Add the tomato basil mix and bake until the cheese melts completely. Let the mushrooms get slightly cooked , then serve.

Mediterranean Seafood Grill with Skordalia

Takes 40-55 minutes to prepare | renders 4 servings)

Ingredients

1. 1 pound russet or Yukon gold potatoes, peeled and diced
2. 8 garlic cloves, peeled
3. 1 slice sourdough bread, crust removed, and torn into pieces
4. 1/4 cup plain low-fat Greek yogurt
5. 3 tablespoons olive oil, divided Zest and juice of 1 lemon
6. 1/2 teaspoon salt, divided
7. 1/4 teaspoon dried thyme
8. 1 pound halibut fillets, cut into 4 pieces
9. 2 red bell peppers, quartered
10. 1 pound small zucchini, diagonally cut into 1-inch pieces
11. 1/2 red onion, sliced

Directions

1. Place potatoes in a big saucepan. Add garlic and some cold water, bring to the boil, and cook for 15 minutes over high heat.

2. While the potatoes get cooked, place the bread in a large bowl. Scoop 2-3 tbsps of cooking liquid from the potatoes over the bread and stir.

3. Stir in yogurt, 2 tbsp of olive oil lemon zest and lemon juice; stir until a smooth paste forms.

4. Drain the potatoes and garlic in the cooking liquid. Now, mash the drained potatoes with the bread mixture. Add the cooking liquid for consistency, followed by about ¼ teaspoon salt and 2 teaspoons olive oil.

5. Pre- heat the grill pan to medium. Brush the fish with 1/2 teaspoon olive oil, and sprinkle with 1/4 teaspoon salt and thyme.

6. Cook for around 2-3 minutes on each side and transfer it to a plate. Make sure it is kept warm until then.

7. Evenly distribute the bell pepper, zucchini, red onion, 1/2 teaspoon olive oil onto the fish in the grill pan and cook for about 5 minutes. Add the zucchini and onion and cook it for a further 10 minutes.

8. Serve halibut with grilled vegetables and skordalia .

Portobello Mushrooms with Mediterranean Stuffing

Takes 40-45 minutes to prepare | renders 4 servings)

Ingredients

1. 4 (4-inch) portobello caps (about 3/4 pound)
2. 1/4 cup finely chopped onion
3. 1/4 cup finely chopped celery
4. 1/4 cup finely chopped carrot
5. 1/4 cup finely chopped red bell pepper
6. 1/4 cup finely chopped green bell pepper
7. 1/4 teaspoon dried Italian seasoning
8. 2 garlic cloves, minced
9. Cooking spray
10. 3 cups (1/4-inch) cubed French bread, toasted
11. 1/2 cup vegetable broth
12. 1/2 cup (2 ounces) feta cheese, crumbled
13. 3 tablespoons low-fat balsamic vinaigrette, divided
14. 4 teaspoons grated fresh Parmesan cheese
15. 1/4 teaspoon black pepper
16. 4 cups mixed salad greens

Description

1. Pre-heat the oven to 350-degrees

2. Remove enough mushroom stems to measure ¼ cup. Place on a bowl and add to the onion, celery, carrot, red bell pepper, green bell pepper, Italian seasoning and garlic.
3. Heat a large skillet to medium, coat the pan with cooking spray, and place the the onion mix in it. Cook for 10 minutes.
4. Combine with the bread using a large bowl, and toss it. Add feta.
5. Use a spoon to scoop out the brown gills from the mushroom caps. Discard the gills. Brush the mushrooms evenly with 1 tablespoon vinaigrette.
6. Add some parmesan and black pepper and top each mushroom with ½ cup of bread mixture.
7. Place on a baking tray and bake until the mushrooms are tender.
8. Add the remaining vinaigrette and greens and toss gently .

Mediterranean Breakfast Couscous

Takes 3-5 minutes to prepare | renders 4 servings)

Ingredients

1. 3 cups 1% low-fat milk
2. 1 (2-inch long) cinnamon sck
3. 1 cup uncooked whole-wheat couscous
4. 1/2 cup chopped dried apricots
5. 1/4 cup dried currants
6. 6 teaspoons dark brown sugar, divided
7. 1/4 teaspoon salt
8. 4 teaspoons butter, melted and divided

Description

1. Pour the milk into a large saucepan over medium to high heat. Add the cinnamon stick and keep heat even at medium to high for three minutes or until bubbles form around the edge. Do not allow to boil.
2. Remove from heat and stir after adding couscous, apricots, currants, 4 teaspoons brown sugar, and salt.

3. Cover the mixture and leave for 15 minutes, then remove and discard the cinnamon stick.

4. Divide the couscous into 4 bowls, top each bowl with some melted buer and ½ tsp brown sugar and serve .

Chicken-Garbanzo Salad

Takes 20-25 minutes to prepare | renders 4 servings)

Ingredients

1. 1 (9-ounce) package frozen cooked chopped chicken breast, thawed
2. 1 (15-ounce) can chickpeas (garbanzo beans), rinsed and drained
3. 1 cup chopped seeded cucumber (about 1 small cucumber)
4. 1/2 cup chopped green onions (about 4 small onions)
5. 1/4 cup chopped fresh mint or basil
6. 1/2 cup plain fat-free yogurt
7. 2 garlic cloves, minced
8. 1/4 teaspoon salt
9. 2 cups prepackaged baby spinach leaves
10. 1/3 cup (1.3 ounces) feta cheese with cracked pepper, crumbled
11. 4 lemon wedges

Directions

1. Combine the first 8 ingredients on the list and toss it gently for a great combination.
2. Add spinach leaves and feta cheese.
3. Toss gently, add some pepper toppings, and serve.
☐

Black-eyed Pea Fritters From West Africa

Takes 30-35 minutes to prepare | renders 8 servings

Ingredients

1. 1 pound dried black-eyed peas
2. 4 cups water, or enough to cover the beans to soak overnight
3. ¾ cup chopped shallots or onion
4. 2 tablespoons chopped garlic (optional)
5. Salt
6. ¼ teaspoon black pepper
7. 3 tablespoons unrefined coconut oil

Directions

1. Keep the black-eyed peas soaked over-night. The next day, drain and peel off the skin. Add some water and rinse again.
2. Place the peas in a blender or food processor and make into a fine paste. Place in a separate bowl when done.
3. Add onions and garlic with a pinch of salt and black pepper.
4. In a skillet, heat oil to medium heat. Form the accara mix into lemon-sized balls. Fry in the oil and keep flipping over for around 5-7 minutes.

5. Fry the accara in small batches. Once it turns brown, remove from the oil using a slotted spoon and place the acara in a plate.
6. Pour some hot sauce over the dish and serve at room temperature.

☐

Yucatan Bean And Pumpkin Seed Appetizer

Takes 15 minutes to prepare | renders 8 servings

Ingredients

1. ¼ cup hulled pumpkin seeds (pepitas)
2. 1 can (15 ½ ounces) white beans, rinsed and drained
3. 1 tomato, finely chopped
4. ⅓ cup white, yellow, or red onion, finely chopped
5. ⅓ cup finely chopped cilantro
6. 3-4 tablespoons lime juice
7. Salt
8. Ground black pepper

Description

1. Place the pumpkin seeds into a small skillet. Heat to medium while continually shaking the pan. Continue this for 3 minutes. Transfer to a bowl and let it cool.
2. Chop with the help of a food processor. If you don't have access to a food processor, a sharp knife should do.

3. Place the pumpkin in a medium sized bowl together with beans, tomatoes, onions, cilantro, and lime juice.
4. Add some salt, pepper and lime juice and serve.

Mediterranean Halibut Sandwiches

Takes 40-50 minutes to prepare | renders 4 servings

Ingredients

Fish
1. Vegetable oil cooking spray
2. 1 (12-ounce) or 2 (6-ounce) center-cut halibut fillets, skinned
3. 1/2 teaspoon kosher salt
4. 1/4 teaspoon freshly ground black pepper
5. Extra-virgin olive oil, for drizzling

Bread
6. 1 loaf ciabatta bread, ends trimmed, halved lengthwise
7. 2 tablespoons extra-virgin olive oil
8. 1 clove garlic, peeled and halved

Filling
9. 1/3 cup mayonnaise
10. 1/4 cup chopped sun-dried tomatoes
11. 1/4 cup chopped fresh basil leaves
12. 2 tablespoons chopped fresh parsley leaves
13. 1 tablespoon capers, drained
14. Zest of 1 large lemon
15. 1/2 teaspoon kosher salt

16. 1/4 teaspoon freshly ground black pepper
17. 2 cups arugula

Directions

1. Place an oven rack in the centre of the oven. pre-heat the oven to 450-degree F.
2. Spray a baking sheet with some veg-oil cooking spray. Place the fish on the tray.
3. Add salt and pepper to taste. Bake until the fish is cooked, for about 10-15 minutes, and let it stand aside for 20 minutes.
4. Pre-heat the grill pan and a large skillet to medium. Brush the sides of the bread with some olive oil. Grill the bread and rub the cooked end with some garlic.
5. Place mayonnaise, sun-dried tomatoes, parsley, basil, capers, lemon zest, salt, and pepper in a medium-sized bowl.
6. Flake the cooked fish and add the filling. Top with some arugula, cut into 4 equal pieces and serve

Conclusion

Thoughts of the Mediterranean bring to mind images of outstretched lazy lunches, loaded with fresh produce. Juicy red tomatoes, warm ciabatta, carafes of wine and rich virgin olive oil stacked to capacity on a long table set in a grove of sun-ripe olives...
Or it can be set in a noisy, chaotic, farmhouse kitchen chock-full of friends and family; a loving family occasion...
with a bright array of colored dishes filled with tzatziki and hummus cheese and el dente pasta dripping with delicious sauces at ones disposal, one finds it difficult to choose from these varying dishes of delightful and mouth-watering, yet healthy and nutritionally balanced, Mediterranean dishes.
Generally low in processed foods, the Mediterranean Cuisine health benefits are derived from an abundance of prime-cut meats, and freshly caught fish, and a cornucopia of freshly harvested vegies and delectable salads. Cheesy side dishes whole grain breads served with olive oil and. It is the pride and delight of the Mediterranean cook to lavish his dishes with garlic and fresh herbs in order to compliment the already taste bud-teasing cuisine and thereby creating some much-loved tastes across the Globe. Grilling

these foods contributes to the wholesomeness of this type of diet... or you may simply enjoy them raw...

The Mediterranean style of cooking includes a combination of styles from countries that are situated around the Mediterranean Ocean.

Sweet and tangy spices from Turkey and Lebanon, rich and salty meats from Spain, creamy Italian mozzarella contrasting with briny Greek olives, all hold an important place on the menu.

However palatable, though, it is not merely the ingredients in the food that make the diet so special.

In the Mediterranean, eating has over decades and even centuries been developed into a relaxation ritual that plays an essential role in the enjoyment of meals. A gathering of family and friends together is as much form of entertainment by means of a leisurely occasion as it is about sustaining the body.

Enjoying one another's company is just as important as savoring the dishes. Many hours can be spent around the lunch- or dinner table. Sharing dishes among various families, each bringing their own to share with others, is common practice. Small plates may be supplied, and guests would take as little- or as much as they would like. This is a wholesome practice that sustains the body as well as strengthens family- and friendship bonds. Their style of eating seems to be one of the reasons why the Mediterranean people are so delightfully laid-back, relaxed and out-going. And being relaxed contributes to being healthy.

All rights Reserved. No part of this publication or the information in it may be quoted from or reproduced in any form by means such as printing, scanning, photocopying or otherwise without prior written permission of the copyright holder.

Disclaimer and Terms of Use: Effort has been made to ensure that the information in this book is accurate and complete, however, the author and the publisher do not warrant the accuracy of the information, text and graphics contained within the book due to the rapidly changing nature of science, research, known and unknown facts and internet. The Author and the publisher do not hold any responsibility for errors, omissions or contrary interpretation of the subject matter herein. This book is presented solely for motivational and informational purposes only.

Thank you

CPSIA information can be obtained
at www.ICGtesting.com
Printed in the USA
LVHW05s1810170618
581007LV00042B/2653/P